1. Abe...
2. Abe...
3. Arra...
4. Argy...
5. Sout...
6. The Borders
7. The Cairngorms
8. Caithness & Sutherland
9. Dumfries and Galloway
10. Dundee & Angus
11. Edinburgh
12. Fife, Kinross & Clackmannan
13. Glasgow
14. Inverness

20. Moray
21. Mull & Iona
22. Orkney
23. The Outer Hebrides
24. Perthshire
25. Ross & Cromarty
26. Royal Deeside
27. Shetland
28. Stirling & The Trossachs

The remaining three books, Caledonia, Distinguished Distilleries and Scotland's Mountains, feature locations throughout the country so are not included in the above list.

PICTURING SCOTLAND

EDINBURGH

NESS PUBLISHING

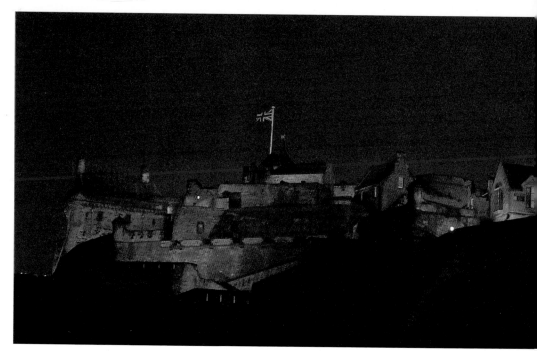

2   Edinburgh Castle at night.

EDINBURGH

Welcome to Edinburgh

Fàilte (welcome) to Edinburgh, the capital of Scotland and one of the most beautiful cities in the world. This is a multi-faceted city, one of hidden depths, elegant vistas, stark contrasts and continual surprises. It is Scotland's centre of government, medicine, law, finance and tourism. Also important are the manufacturing industries of brewing, electronics and publishing. This book will give you a fascinating insight into what is a truly capital city.

Edinburgh's Origins

'Edinburgh was in 1845 a picturesque, odorous, inconvenient, old fashioned town of about 70,000 inhabitants' (Chambers). However, the story begins much earlier with the Castle Rock first fortified during Roman times, taking the name 'Dunedin' meaning 'Hill Fort'. In 1436 the city became capital of Scotland and continued to thrive until the Union with England in 1707 when its importance diminished as the aristocracy moved south. However, the 18th century also heralded a revival in fortunes with the 'Edinburgh Enlightenment' – an era of building and flourishing of the arts and sciences. Today the city continues to expand and prosper and to discard its sobriquet of 'Auld Reekie'. The aerial picture opposite serves as a map of the centre of Edinburgh. It shows how the character of the New Town on the left differs from the Old Town on the right, the two halves separated by Princes Street Gardens. The enclosing high points of the castle (right), Arthur's Seat (top right) and Calton Hill (upper left) can all be clearly seen.

4

This picture shows George Street's central position in the New Town (left), running from the green of Charlotte Square straight up to St Andrew Square.

5

The Castle

Towering 133m/437ft above Edinburgh, perched on a crag of volcanic basalt, the Castle dominates the skyline with breathtaking views over the city and the Firth of Forth beyond. The Castle itself is a gathering of buildings and fortifications, covering seven acres, dating from the early 12th century. The obvious defensive strengths of the site led to James III establishing it as the seat of the Scottish monarchy in 1460.

Today, the Castle houses 'The Honours of Scotland' (the Scottish Crown Jewels), the Stone of Destiny (the ancient Scottish Coronation throne), St Margaret's Chapel (the oldest building in the city), Mons Meg (a massive six ton cannon built in 1449) – and the 'one o'clock gun' which is fired daily. It is also home to the Scottish National War Memorial.

Edinburgh Castle has many fascinating (and some grisly) stories to tell. In the early 1300s it was occupied by the English, but was liberated by a daring night attack led by Sir Thomas Randolph. This involved 30 hand-picked men scaling the near-vertical north face of the castle crag and taking the garrison by surprise.

In 1440 it was the scene of a dastardly political assassination when Sir William Crichton, Keeper of the Castle, invited the teenage Earl of Douglas and his younger brother to a feast (now known as 'The Black Dinner') and afterwards had them beheaded on a trumped-up charge of treason.

Mary, Queen of Scots gave birth to Prince James at the castle in 1566. He became King James VI of Scotland and James I of England.

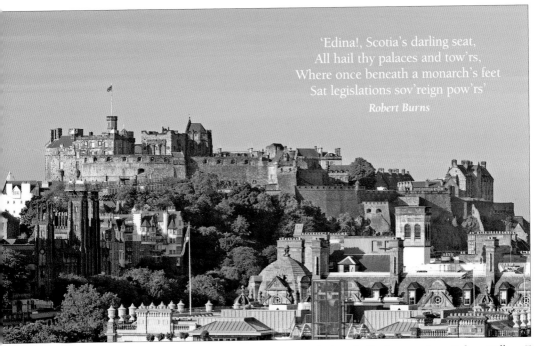

'Edina!, Scotia's darling seat,
All hail thy palaces and tow'rs,
Where once beneath a monarch's feet
Sat legislations sov'reign pow'rs'
Robert Burns

Edinburgh Castle seen from Calton Hill. 7

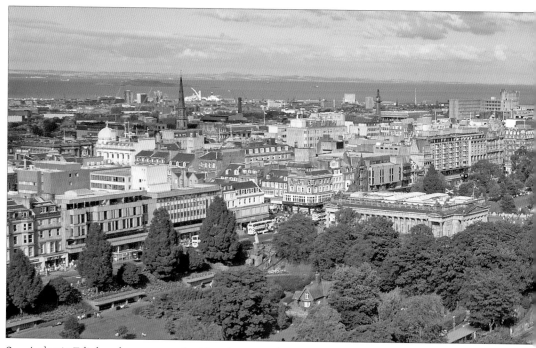

8 A classic Edinburgh panorama, looking down on the New Town from the castle. The National Gallery of Scotland is on The Mound, above the railway tunnel entrance at the bottom of the picture.

10 Left: the exterior of the Scottish National War Memorial, Edinburgh Castle. Right: The Royal Palace faces on to Crown Square in the castle. Mary, Queen of Scots, gave birth to the future King James VI here.

For many, attending the Royal Edinburgh Military Tattoo is the highlight of a visit to Edinburgh. Set against the world-famous backdrop of Edinburgh Castle, the Tattoo features awe-inspiring colour and variety.

12 St Margaret's Chapel (the oldest part of the castle and the oldest building in Edinburgh), and the St Margaret window, inside the chapel.

From the castle at top left, the Royal Mile bisects the Old Town, running down to Holyrood and the 13 new Scottish Parliament building at bottom right.

The Old Town

'… that in no city in the world so many people live in so little room as in Edinburgh' *Daniel Defoe*

The 'Royal Mile' is the backbone of Edinburgh's Old Town, with numerous closes and wynds (lanes) branching off it at right angles, giving the appearance of a fish's skeleton from the air.

This is an area steeped in history, housing the largest concentration of historic buildings in Britain, including the medieval townhouse dedicated to John Knox. Lady Stair's House (1622) is now a writers' museum commemorating Robert Burns, Sir Walter Scott and Robert Louis Stevenson. The Tron Kirk (church) is named after the public weighing beam which used to stand outside.

The original Old Town extended from the Castle to the protective city walls at the Netherbow Port. Residents seldom ventured beyond these walls, with the last close in the Netherbow aptly named 'World's End'.

Due to limited space, the 'lands' (high tenements) grew upwards rather than outwards, to as many as 16 storeys and led to Edinburgh being the original city of skyscrapers. Within these 'lands' all classes of society rubbed shoulders, from the aristocracy to the working classes. The well-to-do occupied the lower floors while the poor huddled in the exposed upper storeys.

The 'Mile' thronged with stalls and 'luckenbooths' (lockable shops) and today many of the closes still bear the name of the trade carried out there – Fishmarket, Fleshmarket, Bakehouse, to name but a few.

The Camera Obscura and World of Illusions, left, has the most powerful public telescope in Britain 15 and provides panoramic views over the city, such as this one looking north over the Firth of Forth.

16 Lawnmarket is part of the Royal Mile. Numerous wynds lead off to the many courts of tenements behind, such as this entry to Milnes Court.

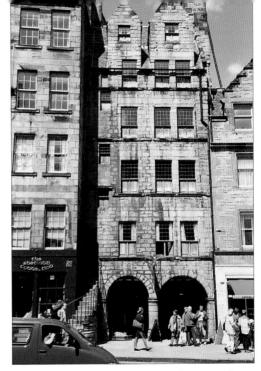

Left: looking down the Royal Mile. Right: Gladstone's Land, a restored merchant's house and booth, built 1617. Situated in the Lawnmarket, it belonged to Thomas Gledstane.

18 The National Library of Scotland is just off the Royal Mile on George IV Bridge. It presents a programme of exhibitions; this is part of the John Murray Archive Exhibition, a permanent display.

St Giles 'Cathedral'

Located on the High Street section of the Royal Mile and on the site of an earlier Celtic church, St Giles is the High Kirk (Parish Church) of Edinburgh and dates from 1124. A place of worship for nearly 900 years, the church has also faced war, fire and hatred. It has separated friends and re-joined enemies, welcomed kings and queens, soldiers, paupers, prisoners and judges. It was here that John Knox (1513-72) played a key role in the Scottish Reformation of the 1550s–1560s which led to the acceptance of Presbyterianism. St Giles contains many fine stained-glass windows, a magnificent organ and the exquisite Thistle Chapel. Officially, it was only a cathedral during two relatively brief periods in the 17th century when the English were trying to impose Episcopalianism on the Scots. However, even today it is still frequently referred to as St Giles Cathedral.

The stained-glass window in the Chepman Aisle of St Giles throws light on to the Marquis of Montrose memorial.

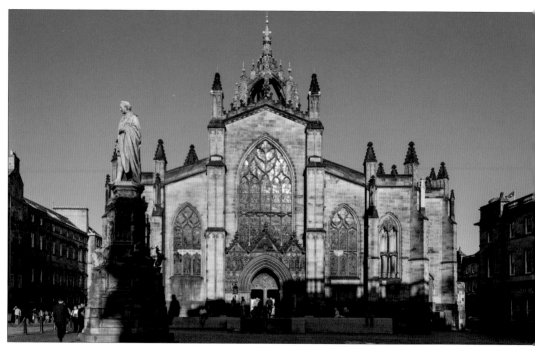

20 West elevation of St Giles High Kirk with statue of Walter Francis Montague Douglas Scott, 2nd Duke of Buccleuch and 7th Duke of Queensferry on the left.

The interior of St Giles High Kirk, looking across the Sanctuary towards the North Window. **21**

22 Left: the extraordinarily ornate Thistle Chapel, spiritual home and meeting place of The Most Ancient and Most Noble Order of the Thistle. Right: detail of two Knights' crests.

Mary King's Close

The scene on the right may not be a place of beauty, but no visitor to Edinburgh (or resident for that matter) should miss this. Hidden beneath the Royal Mile lies Edinburgh's deepest secret: a warren of hidden 'closes' where real people lived, worked and died. For years they have lain forgotten and abandoned. Mary King's Close is where you can experience the sights, sounds and maybe even smells of an amazing street that time forgot, where everyday people went about their day-to-day lives and where you can now walk in their footsteps. This strange, dark underground site is one of four closes that date back to the 1600s. They were not always underground, but were buried beneath later buildings such as the City Chambers. Astonishingly, the houses that became vaults beneath the new structures continued to be inhabited by those who could not afford anywhere else.

24 Victoria Street, leading to West Bow (left) runs down from George IV Bridge to the Grassmarket. Victoria Terrace, above Victoria Street, provides the upper view (centre, top) which looks down to Wes

Bow and the Grassmarket. The lower centre picture provides a close-up of some of this architecture. 25
The picture on the right gives a more thorough view of the Grassmarket and its café culture.

26 Left: John Knox's house, High Street, just down from St Giles High Kirk. Right: you never know who might entertain you on the Royal Mile, especially during the Edinburgh Festival.

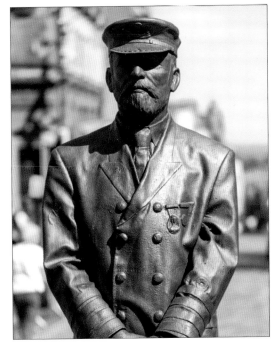

At Festival time (August), many Fringe events take place on the streets. Top left: puppet drummer;
lower left: the Dark Jokes make great music; right: a human statue waits to surprise his next victim!

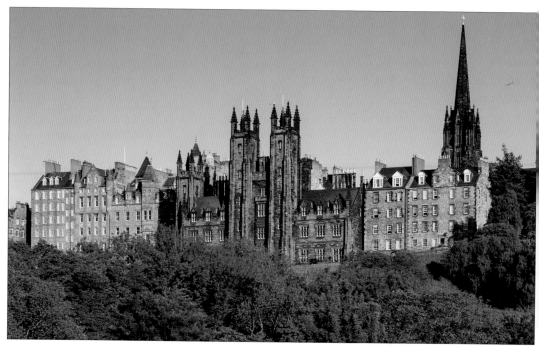

28 A view of the Old Town from Princes Street Gardens, with the twin towers of the Free Church's New College in the centre. The Church of Scotland Assembly Hall is further back in this complex.

Some Edinburgh legends

Burke and Hare – 'bodysnatchers' who murdered 16 people to feed the demand for bodies for anatomy demonstrations at the city's medical school.

Deacon Brodie – a town councillor and pillar of the community by day but a daring cat burglar by night and the inspiration for Dr Jekyll and Mr Hyde

Greyfriars Bobby – a loyal Skye terrier who guarded his master's grave for 14 years and was cared for by local residents, is commemorated in the statue at the top of Candlemaker Row.

Mary King's Close – a busy thoroughfare off the High Street which was sealed off in 1645 to prevent the spread of the plague. Fear and superstition haunt the Close to this day.

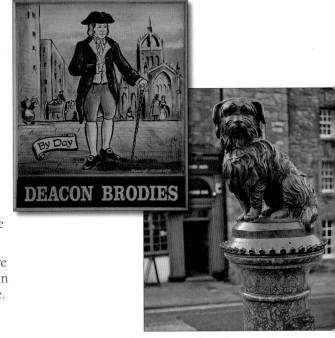

The sign outside Deacon Brodie's Tavern and the statue of Greyfriars Bobby. **29**

30 Access to Greyfriars Church is from near Greyfriars Bobby. Opened in 1620, it is famed as the place where the National Covenant was signed in 1638.

This is the George Buchanan window inside Greyfriars Church. In 1570 Buchanan was appointed **31** tutor to the young king James VI and until 1578 also held the office of Lord Privy Seal.

32 What we now know as the National Museum of Scotland opened in these purpose-built premises on Chambers Street in 1866. This is the appropriately named Grand Gallery.

Two of the Museum's more significant exhibits are, left, the Lewis Chessmen of which these are **33** two pieces and, right, Bonnie Prince Charlie's travelling canteen.

34 The modern part of the museum, opened in 1998 and seen above, adjoins the original building and between them they recount the story of all things made, used and found in Scotland.

Edinburgh University

The 'Tounis College' was established in 1583 by the Town Council. The present 'Old Quad' with its imposing dome topped by the statue of the Golden Boy (see opposite), was designed by Robert Adam in 1789 and is considered his most impressive work. The Greek revival interiors are all by William Playfair and his 200ft long upper library is easily one of the grandest neo-classical rooms in Britain. The University itself is internationally famous, particularly in medicine, law and divinity. Edinburgh can boast three other Universities, Heriot-Watt, Napier and Queen Margaret.

Celebrated ex-students include the writers Thomas Carlyle, Robert Louis Stevenson, Sir Walter Scott, Sir Arthur Conan Doyle and Peter Mark Roget. Others include Prof. James Simpson, Charles Darwin, James Hutton and John Witherspoon (signatory of the American Declaration of Independence).

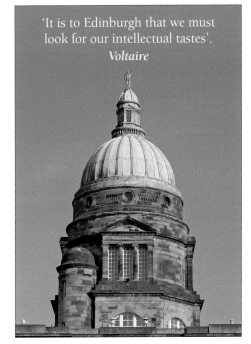

'It is to Edinburgh that we must look for our intellectual tastes'.
Voltaire

36 William Playfair designed the 200ft-long upper library in the University, which is easily one of the grandest neo-classical rooms in Britain.

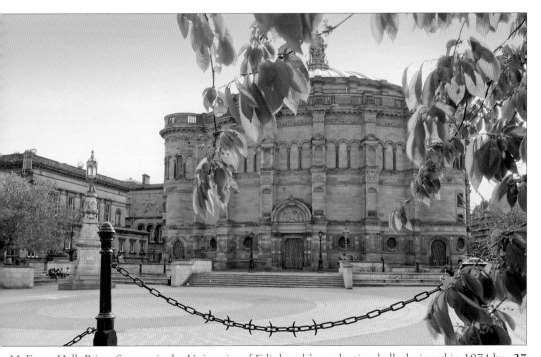

McEwan Hall, Bristo Square, is the University of Edinburgh's graduation hall, designed in 1874 by
Sir Robert Rowand Anderson. The inside imitates a Greek theatre with two tiers of galleries.

38 Just south of the University, the Meadows provide a recreational space of playing fields and tree-lined avenues, much enjoyed by the student population.

Returning now to the Royal Mile, the lower part of which is called Canongate, where the Tolbooth houses The People's Story. On the left, the Museum of Edinburgh is located in Huntly House.

40 At the tail of the Royal Mile lies the magnificent Baroque Palace of Holyroodhouse; the name 'Holy Rood' or 'Holy Cross' refers to the original Abbey built on the site in 1128. The first Palace was built in 1503 by James IV and added to by successive monarchs. Today it remains the official residence of the Royal Family in Scotland and is part of the Royal Collection Trust.

42 Left: Canongate Kirk, the building of which was ordained by King James VII in 1688.
Right: Holyrood is at the bottom of Canongate, where stands the Abbey Sanctuary building.

Close to Holyrood, just off Canongate, the historic enclave of White Horse Close dates back to 1623.

44 Fronting on to Abbey Strand, Holyrood, this is the southern side of the oldest part of Abbey Sanctuary, built in the early 16th century. The adjoining West Building is seen on p.42.

his east-Edinburgh view shows the layout of the Holyrood area with Our Dynamic Earth t the bottom, the Scottish Parliament above it and Holyrood Palace to the right.

46 A closer look at the new Scottish Parliament building, showing the distinctive shapes that have attracted so much attention.

Calton Hill from Salisbury Crags with the incomplete National Monument in the centre, the 30m/100ft- 47 high Calton Tower to its left and the former Royal High School below. The Firth of Forth lies beyond.

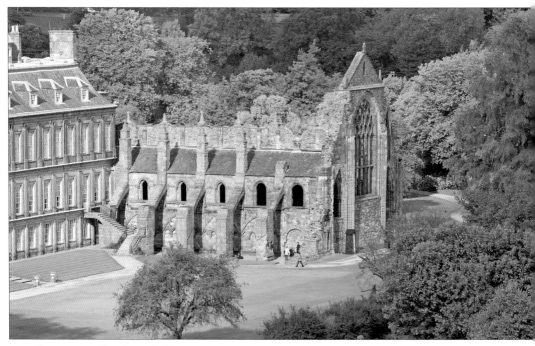

48 The remains of Holyrood Abbey seen from Salisbury Crags (part of the Arthur's Seat formations). King David I founded the Abbey, reputedly in gratitude for miraculously surviving a hunting accident

Now from within the grounds of Holyrood Abbey, the east window seen opposite throws **49** its shadow on the footings of the more extensive structure that once stood here.

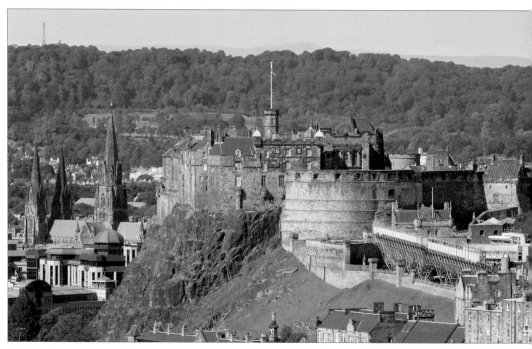

50 On these pages we have an interesting contrast: above is a long-lens view of Edinburgh Castle taken from Salisbury Crags, with Corstorphine Hill to the west of the city in the background …

... while *from* Corstorphine Hill this wintry scene takes in the opposite aspect, with the Castle at **51** upper left and Salisbury Crags just visible through the snow at upper right.

52 At the eastern end of the Arthur's Seat/Salisbury Crags outcrops are the remains of the early 15th-century St Anthony's Chapel. The port of Leith is in the distance.

The peaceful beauty of St Margaret's Loch, below Arthur's Seat, **53**
with St Anthony's Chapel on the skyline.

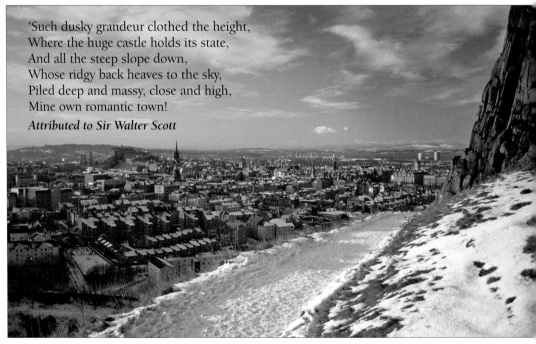

'Such dusky grandeur clothed the height,
Where the huge castle holds its state,
And all the steep slope down,
Whose ridgy back heaves to the sky,
Piled deep and massy, close and high,
Mine own romantic town!

Attributed to Sir Walter Scott

Another view from Salisbury Crags, a wintry scene looking towards the city centre.

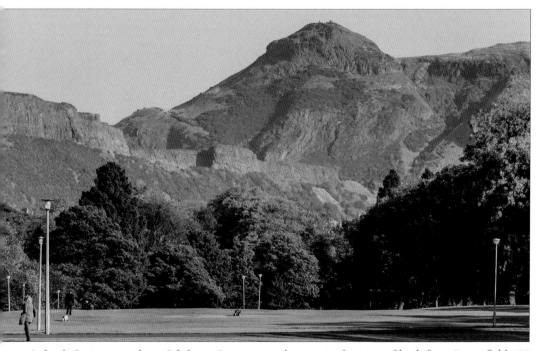

Arthur's Seat towers above Salisbury Crags, as can be seen in this view of both from Bruntsfield **55** Links (home to one of Edinburgh's oldest golf clubs) on the south side of the city.

56 Calton Hill stands at the east end of the New Town and provides an ideal vantage point from which to see the city, especially when sunset silhouettes the skyline. The monument on the right is a

memorial to the Scottish philosopher Dugald Stewart (1753–1828). The Castle is on the left with the tower of The Balmoral Hotel to its right.

58 Newhailes House, near Musselburgh, is a dignified 17th-century mansion with 18th-century additions. It is in the care of the National Trust for Scotland and open to the public.

Craigmillar Castle is one of the best-preserved castles in Scotland. It was begun in the early **59** 15th century, the earliest part being the L-shaped tower which can be seen in the picture.

60 As we turn our attention to the New Town, we take one last look at the Old Town, specifically the magnificent houses of Ramsay Gardens, as seen from Princes Street in the new city.

Edinburgh's New Town, with Moray Place, Ainslie Place and Randolph Crescent **61** from left to right at the bottom of the picture.

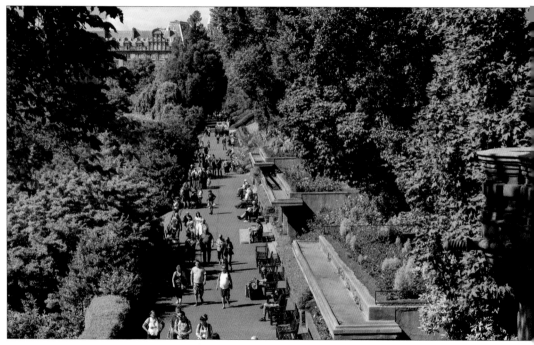

62 Edinburgh's famous Princes Street Gardens. They fill the valley between the Old and New Towns that used to contain the Nor' Loch (see page 76).

This cottage was built for the head gardener of West Princes Street Gardens as part of **63** a re-development that took place from 1876. The West Gardens cover 29 acres.

64 Floral Clock, Princes Street Gardens – up to 40,000 plants make this the largest clock of its kind in the world. It is also the oldest.

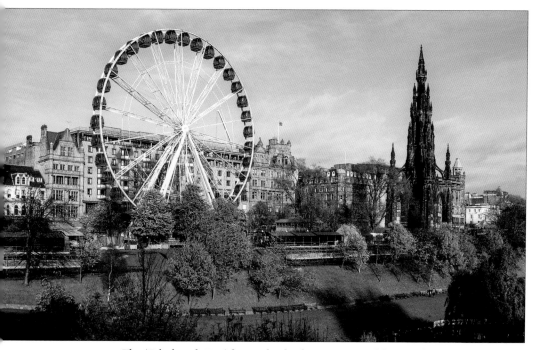

The 'Edinburgh Eye' ferris wheel is being prepared for its Christmas season, **65** while booths for the Christmas Market are being set up in this November view.

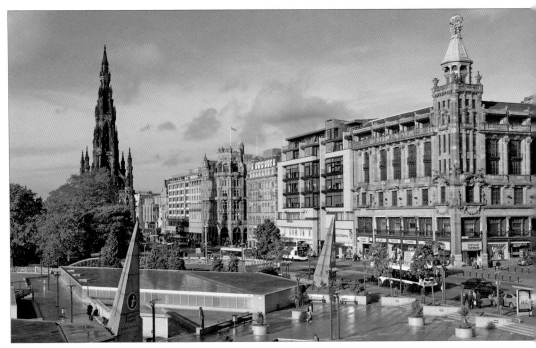

66 Princes Street itself, seen from The Balmoral Hotel. The Scott Monument stands tall on the left, across the street from Jenners, Edinburgh's premier department store.

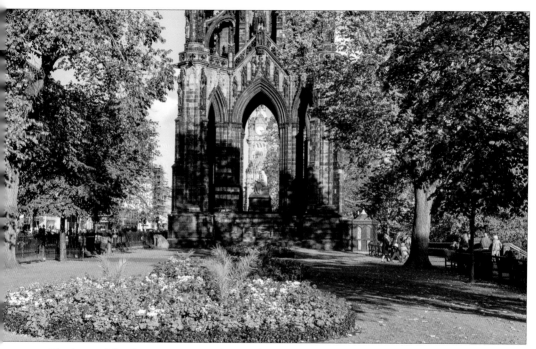

The base of the Scott Monument frames the tower of The Balmoral Hotel. Now it's time to
climb the Monument and see how the city looks from this superb vantage point . . .

68 From aloft, the National Gallery of Scotland takes centre stage. Located on The Mound, this neo-classical building houses an outstanding collection of works ranging from the renaissance to contemporary artists.

The Mound at night, with the National Gallery of Scotland on the right. **69**
The Bank of Scotland building is on the left.

70 Edinburgh's massive Waverley Station fills the valley between the old and new towns. In the distance and against a stormy sky, Arthur's Seat and Salisbury Crags demonstrate their proximity to the city.

The lights of The Balmoral Hotel, North Bridge and Waverley station illuminate the Edinburgh night sky.

72 Again from high up in the Scott Monument, this view is the opposite of the one seen on pages 8-9. The commanding position of the Castle is seen to good effect. To its right, the long reddish building

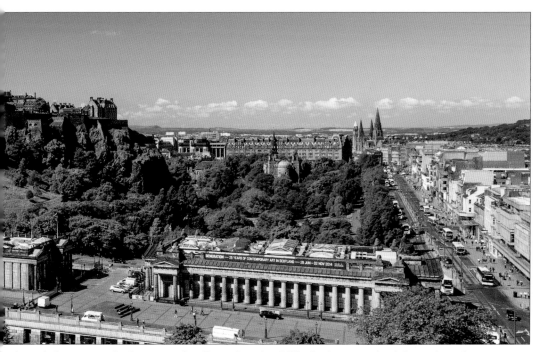

is the Caledonian Hotel. The National Gallery of Scotland fills the foreground, while on the right
Princes Street stretches away to the West End.

74 An unusual view of one of Edinburgh's new trams, which run from the Airport to York Place in the New Town. Right: a tranquil autumn moment in Princes Street Gardens.

The length of Princes Street as seen from Calton Hill with the tower of the Balmoral Hotel on the left. **75**
The three spires of St Mary's Episcopal Cathedral pierce the sky beyond.

The New Town

Plans for Edinburgh's New Town were first proposed in 1752 before James Craig's grid-iron plan of three main streets with squares at either end was finally accepted in 1766. Work on this, the first New Town, was completed in 1791. It was not long before building work began on a second New Town, just to the north, in 1802.

The development of the New Town – the largest area of Georgian urban development in the world – led to 'the great flit' away from the squalor and slums of the Old Town. The Nor' Loch, by this time a polluted and unhealthy lake, was drained to form Princes Street Gardens and the steep causeway of The Mound, connecting Old and New Towns, was completed from the earth dug from the foundations of the New Town. Most of the buildings were constructed using sandstone from the city's Craigleith quarry, once the largest in Scotland.

This golden age of building culminated with the still incomplete National Monument on Calton Hill; supposedly representing the Parthenon, it earned Edinburgh the nickname 'the Athens of the North'. Today the New Town remains an architectural and environmental gem, comprising over 11,000 listed buildings, with many still in residential use. The house pictured is typical of this part of Edinburgh.

Left: fine architecture in George Street. Right upper: The Abbotsford is known as one of Edinburgh's 'poets' pubs'. Right lower: one of the entrances to Edinburgh's principal department store.

78 St Andrew Square, laid out in 1768, is at the eastern end of George Street. The column in the picture is the Melville Monument, in memory of Henry Dundas, the 1st Viscount Melville.

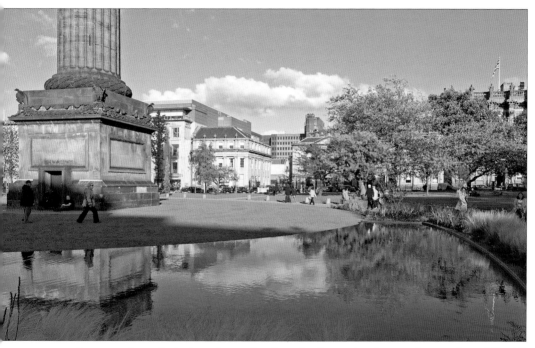

In recent times, St Andrew Square has been landscaped and opened up to the public **79** so everyone can enjoy this lovely space in its remodelled form.

80 Left: the Walter Scott Monument, Princes Street – climb the 287 steps to the top of this 61m/200ft gothic memorial. Right: statue of the Duke of Wellington situated at Waterloo Place.

Calton Hill: right of Hamilton's Obelisk is the Dugald Stewart monument, partly hiding **81** Observatory House. The City Observatory is in the centre. The Governor's House is on the right.

82 The Georgian House – situated in Charlotte Square, this magnificently restored property shows how a prosperous Edinburgh family lived around 1800. Right: the sumptuous Dining Room.

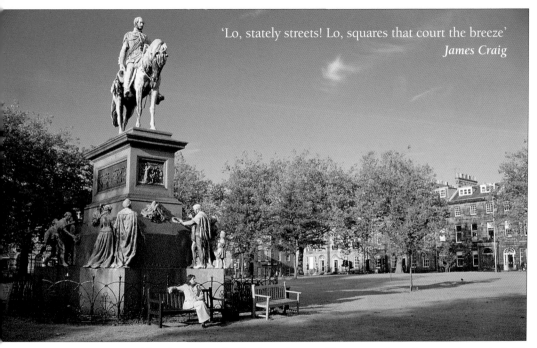

'Lo, stately streets! Lo, squares that court the breeze'
James Craig

Prince Albert's memorial, Charlotte Square. This square is at the opposite end of George Street from St Andrew Square.

84　Now to Edinburgh's West End, where an interesting contrast in circular buildings competes for our attention. The Usher Hall on Lothian Road is one of Edinburgh's foremost concert venues …

... while just a few hundred yards away on Morrison Street, the Edinburgh International Conference **85**
Centre (EICC) is one of the city's defining buildings of modern times.

86 Also at the West End are St Cuthbert's Church (see also p.112) on the left with St John's to its right A very fine traditional carousel is also in evidence, often located here in summer.

St Mary's Episcopal Cathedral

Situated in the West End of Edinburgh's New Town, St Mary's is the cathedral of the Scottish Episcopal Church and is considered to be the architect Sir George Gilbert Scott's masterpiece. Its existence also owes much to two sisters, Barbara and Mary Walker, who donated the site and much of the money needed for its construction. While it is relatively recent (being consecrated in 1879), it reflects 13th-century style and echoes the ruined abbeys of Kelso and Jedburgh. With three spires and set amid fine lawns, St Mary's creates an image of power and elegance. The Cathedral is unique in Scotland in maintaining daily sung services and is noted for its choir school.

88 Salisbury Crags and Arthur's Seat seen from the Pentland Hills. Salisbury Crags' 30m/100ft-high cliff of columnar basalt called 'Samson's Ribs' (left) can be seen to good effect. Arthur's Seat, the 251m/823ft

extinct 'Edinburgh volcano' (right) last erupted over 325million years ago. The surrounding Holyrood
Park, extending to over 650 acres, is one of the grandest open city spaces anywhere in the world.

90 Just north of the West End, Dean Village is tucked away in the steep valley of the Water of Leith. The village grew as a milling settlement, utilising the energy of the river.

Pictured here is Well Court, an innovative housing development completed in 1886. It was commissioned in 1883 by Sir John Findlay, who was then the owner of The Scotsman newspaper.

92 Left: close-up of Well Court showing its stylish architectural touches and some complex roof structures
Right: looking through an entrance to Well Court to cottages on the other side of the river.

High above the village, Dean Bridge carries the main road from Edinburgh to the north. **93**
It was built 1829 – 1831 to designs by Thomas Telford.

94 The Scottish National Gallery of Modern Art is housed at two sites on Belford Road, west of Dean Village. This is Modern One, where Charles Jencks' work of land art *Landform* fills the foreground.

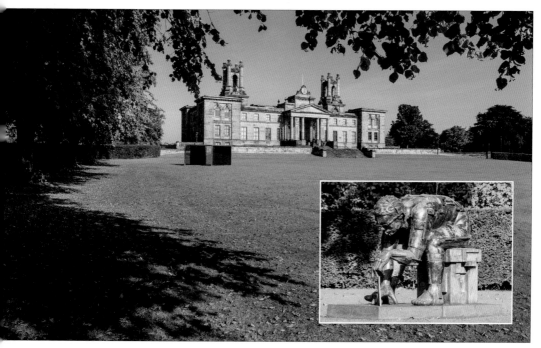

One the other side of Belford Road is Modern Two. Inset: both galleries have exhibits in their **95** grounds; this is *Master of the Universe* by Eduardo Paolozzi at Modern Two.

96 Elegant suburban streets like this one in Stockbridge (just north of the New Town) surround the city. This is where Ann Street, coming in on the left, meets Dean Terrace.

Another example of suburban style: the geometric precision of a gabled terrace in **97** Murrayfield Avenue is framed by foliage in this leafy street.

98 Left: even the basements get the floral treatment. Right: a classical statue at St Bernard's Well between Dean Village and Stockbridge.

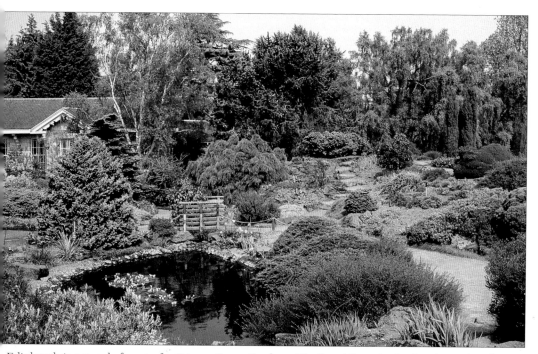

Edinburgh is not only famous for Princes Street Gardens. The Royal Botanic Garden, located to the **99** north of the New Town, is renowned for its informal parklands and formal gardens.

100 The hothouses are home to large numbers of exotic plants, while outside, colourful displays make fine showings throughout much of the year.

This is the Temperate Palm House, built in 1862 as an extension to the earlier Tropical Palm House. **101**
It stands 22m/72ft to the top of the glass dome.

102 Edinburgh is home to many fine schools, past and present. This used to be Donaldson's School for the Deaf at Haymarket, completed in 1851, which at the time of writing is awaiting redevelopment.

Fettes College, in the suburb of Comely Bank, is one of the best-known **103** independent schools in Scotland.

The Royal Yacht *Britannia*

Britannia is one of the world's most famous ships. Launched at John Brown's Shipyard in Clydebank in 1953, the Royal Yacht proudly served Queen and country for 44 years. During that time *Britannia* carried The Queen and the Royal Family on 968 official voyages, from the remotest regions of the South Seas to the deepest divides of Antarctica.

In June 1994, the Government announced that Her Majesty's Yacht *Britannia* would be taken out of service. At the beginning of January 1997, *Britannia* set sail from Portsmouth to Hong Kong on her last and longest voyage. On 11 December 1997 *Britannia* was decommissioned at Portsmouth Naval Base in the presence of The Queen, The Duke of Edinburgh and 14 senior members of the Royal Family. Some 2,200 Royal Yacht Officers and Yachtsmen, together with their families, came to witness the ceremony.

Today's visitors enjoy an extensive and fascinating tour of the vessel, from Bridge to State Rooms to Engine Room!

104 The permanent berthing of the Royal Yacht *Britannia* has provided Leith with a major tourist attraction.

With the atmosphere of a comfortable country house, this is the State Drawing Room on *Britannia*. **105**
The Royal Family hosted many world leaders and other dignitaries here.

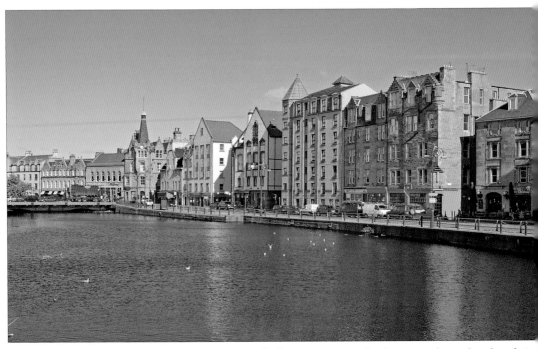

106 Leith, the ancient port of the city, was Scotland's foremost port and a thriving independent burgh in its own right until it amalgamated with its larger neighbour in 1920.

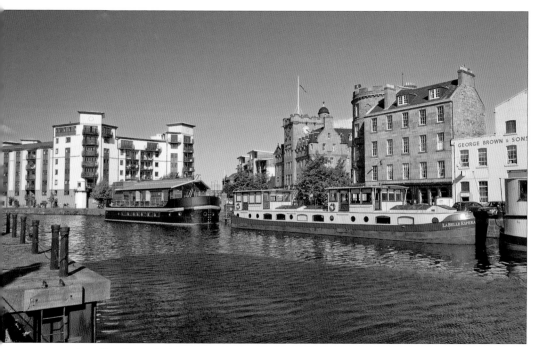

Leith suffered greatly from the decline in its major industries of shipbuilding and fishing. **107**
More recently however, it has seen a revival of its fortunes.

108 The redevelopment of its dockyards, the opening of many new restaurants and bars, increased cruise liner traffic and the new Scottish Government building (above) have all helped.

Lauriston Castle, near Davidson's Mains. Step inside and you will see it just as it was in 1926, **109** when it was left to the nation by the last private owner.

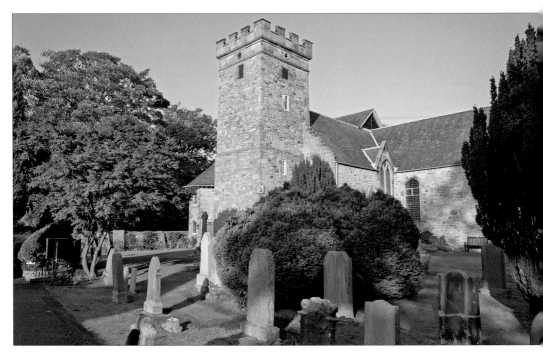

110 The pretty village of Cramond lies just north-west of Edinburgh on the shores of the Firth of Forth. Cramond Kirk dates back to the 15th century.

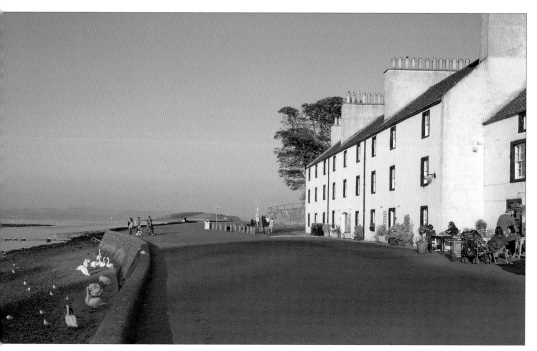

Residents and visitors enjoy a quiet autumn evening on Cramond waterfront. Cramond was 111 originally Caer Amon – the fort on the River Almond, a Roman construction.

'Nisi Dominus Frustra'
('Unless the Lord the
city keeps, the watchmen
watch in vain')
Edinburgh motto

'Coming back to Edinburgh
is to me like coming home'
Charles Dickens

Published 2015 by Ness Publishing, 47 Academy Street, Elgin, Moray, IV30 1LR.
Phone 01343 549663 www.nesspublishing.co.uk
(First edition 2008, second edition 2011 and reprinted 2013 & 2014)

All photographs © Colin and Eithne Nutt except pp.5, 13 & 61 © Guthrie Aerial Photography; p.11 courtesy of 'The Royal Edinburgh Military Tattoo'; pp.12 (right), 17 (left), 24/25 centre top, 29 (both), 53 & 83 © Callum Whyte; p.23 courtesy of The Real Mary King's Close; p.33 (both) © National Museums Scotland; p.36 © Tricia Malley and Ross Gillespie for the University of Edinburgh; p.51 © Duncan MacLaren; pp.54 & 100 © Paul Turner; p.82 (right) © National Trust for Scotland p.85© David Barbour; p.104 © andy gray digital; p.105 © Marc Millar

Text © Callum Dalziel Cochrane and Colin Nutt
ISBN 978-1-906549-61-9

Front cover: Edinburgh panorama from Calton Hill; p.1: Observatory House, Calton Hill; p.4: statue of Sir Walter Scott at the Scott Monument; this page: low-relief frieze of the Last Supper in St Cuthbert's Church; back cover: the unfinished National Monument on Calton Hill

For a list of websites and phone numbers please turn over >

Websites and phone numbers (where available) of featured places in alphabetical order.

Abbey Sanctuary: canmore.rcahms.gov.uk
Camera Obscura: www.camera-obscura.co.uk (T) 0131 226 3709
Canongate Kirk: www.canongatekirk.org.uk (T) 0131 556 3515
Craigmillar Castle: www.historic-scotland.gov.uk (T) 0131 661 4445
Cramond Kirk: www.cramondkirk.org.uk
Edinburgh Castle: www.historic-scotland.gov.uk (T) 0131 225 9846
Edinburgh University: www.ed.ac.uk (T) 0131 650 1000
Gladstone's Land: www.nts.org.uk (T) 0844 493 2120
Greyfriars Bobby: www.greyfriarsbobby.co.uk
Greyfriars Church: www.greyfriarskirk.com (T) 0131 225 1900
Holyrood Abbey: www.historic-scotland.gov.uk (T) 0131 557 2365
Jenners: www.houseoffraser.co.uk (T) 0131 225 2442
Lauriston Castle: www.edinburghmuseums.org.uk (T) 0131 336 2060
Mary King's Close: www.realmarykingsclose.com (T) 0845 070 6244
Museum of Edinburgh: www.edinburghmuseums.org.uk (T) 0131 529 4143
National Library of Scotland: www.nls.uk (T) 0131 623 3700
Nelson Monument (Calton Tower): www.edinburghmuseums.org.uk (T) 0131 556 2716
Newhailes House: www.nts.org.uk (T) 0844 493 2125
Our Dynamic Earth: www.dynamicearth.co.uk (T) 0131 550 7800
Royal Mile: www.royal-mile.com
Scottish National Gallery of Modern Art: www.nationalgalleries.org (T) 0131 624 6200
St Cuthbert's Church: www.st-cuthberts.net (T) 0131 229 1142
St Giles Cathedral: www.stgilescathedral.org.uk (T) 0131 225 9442
St John's Church: www.stjohns-edinburgh.org.uk (T) 0131 225 7565
St Mary's Episcopal Cathedral: www.cathedral.net (T) 0131 225 6293